Baby's Wild Adventure

Shapes and Navigation

Melanie Lago

Susanna Stossel

Catherine Twomey Fosnot

Table of Contents

Unit Overview

The focus of this unit is the early development of children's ideas about shape and measurement. By fostering exploration of the shapes of large-scale, navigable surface layouts and small-scale, movable objects, children are supported to coordinate two core geometries: (1) mapping, comprised of the properties of distance and direction; and (2) shapes, comprised of the properties of number of sides and angles. The unit is designed to align with the CCSS Standards of Practice and the following core objectives:

Measurement and Data K.MD

CCSS.Math.Content.K.M.1 Describe measurable attributes of objects, such as length. Describe several measurable attributes of a single object.

CCSS.Math.Content.K.M.2 Directly compare two objects with a measurable attribute in common, to see which object has "more of"/"less of" the attribute, and describe the difference.

CCSS.Math.Content.K.M.3 Classify objects into given categories; count the number of objects in each category and sort the categories by count.

Geometry K.G

CCSS.Math.Content.K.G.1 Describe objects in the environment using names of shapes, and describe the relative positions of these objects using terms such as *above, below, beside, in front of, behind,* and *next to.*

CCSS.Math.Content.K.G.2 Correctly name shapes regardless of their orientations or overall size.

CCSS.Math.Content.K.G.3 Identify shapes as two-dimensional (lying in a plane, "flat") or three-dimensional ("solid").

CCSS.Math.Content.K.G.4 Analyze and compare two- and three-dimensional shapes, in different sizes and orientations, using informal language to describe their similarities, differences, parts (e.g., number of sides and vertices/"corners") and other attributes (e.g. having sides of equal length).

CCSS.Math.Content.K.G.5 Model shapes in the world by building shapes from components and drawing shapes.

CCSS.Math.Content.K.G.6 Compose simple shapes to form larger shapes.

The unit is comprised of a series of investigations based on the context of a baby's adventure as she explores her backyard. As she navigates around objects in her environment, Baby drops her blanket, yet then finds it again. The setting provides a mystery of how this happened and what shapes she must have navigated around. At first children model the situation temporally, as a line with just a sequence of events, but as they explore further they come to realize that the spaces are enclosed and that the beginning points are the same as the endpoints. In fact, Baby has traversed along a number of straight paths and at the end of each made a turn bringing her back to where she started.

This navigational situation supports children to construct the properties of two dimensional shapes, which then are used to sort and to name polygons. In the second week of the unit, 3-D solids are introduced and children learn to sort them by the shape and number of their faces. The unit culminates with children designing and building new objects (composing and decomposing shapes) and writing their own Baby adventure stories.

The Landscape of Learning

BIG IDEAS
❖ Pathways traveled can be represented as lines on paper with landmarks
❖ Pathways have direction and distance
❖ Pathways can enclose space
❖ The shape of the enclosed space can be analyzed by properties such as distance and turns
❖ Distance and turns are related to angles and lengths of shapes
❖ Shapes are conserved through flips and rotations
❖ Shapes are sorted and named according to their properties
STRATEGIES
❖ Analyzes shapes only as visual objects
❖ Uses borders of the environment traveled to orient
❖ Draws a map as a line of movement with landmarks
❖ Draws and recognizes shapes topologically
❖ Encodes shapes of surface layouts traveled
❖ Draws, analyzes, and sorts shapes using Euclidean properties
❖ Physically rotates objects to prove congruency
❖ Mentally rotates objects to prove congruency
MODELS
❖ Navigation pathways: temporal, topological, Euclidean
❖ 2D shapes
❖ 3D solids

NAVIGATION AND SHAPE

3D solids have faces that are 2D shapes

3D modeling of solids

2D modeling of shapes

With polygons, the number of angles is the same as the number of sides

Uses one line to represent shared boundaries

Shapes can be composed of or decomposed into other shapes

One line can define two bounded areas simultaneously

Mentally rotates objects to prove congruency

Shapes are categorized and named according to their properties

Models navigation with Euclidean properties

Shapes are conserved through flips and rotations

Draws, analyzes, and sorts shapes using Euclidean properties of sides and corners

Physically rotates objects to prove congruency

Distance and turns are related to lengths of sides and angles

Encodes shapes of surface layouts traveled

Models navigation topologically

The shape of the enclosed space can be analyzed by properties such as distance and turns

Draws a map as a line of movement

Pathways can enclose space

Pathways can be represented as lines with landmarks

Models navigation temporally

Draws, recognizes, and sorts shapes topologically

Pathways have direction and distance

Analyzes shapes only as visual objects

Uses borders to orient

The landscape of learning showing landmark strategies (rectangles), big ideas (ovals), and models (triangles).

The Mathematical Landscape

Baby's Adventure is designed to support the development of the coordination of two foundational geometries: (1) navigation and mapping; and (2) the analysis and recognition of shapes. Current research in cognitive development (Spelke, Lee, and Izard, 2011; Dehaene, Izard, Pica, and Spelke, 2006; Davies and Uttal, 2007) suggests that babies have two core cognitive systems: one that guides them as they move and another for the analysis of the shapes of small objects for recognition and categorization. But neither system by itself is sufficient to explain the development of the fundamental Euclidean relationships such as length, angle, and direction, which will be needed for higher-level understandings of geometry. The investigations in this unit involve the drawing of paths traveled, orienting, and the drawing, matching and sorting of 2-D and 3-D shapes to support the productive combination of representations from these two core systems.

BIG IDEAS

As young children explore the investigations within the unit, several big ideas arise. These include:

❖ *Pathways have direction and distance*
❖ *Pathways traveled can be represented as lines with landmarks*
❖ *Pathways can enclose space*
❖ *The shape of the enclosed space can be analyzed by properties such as distance and turns*
❖ *Distance and turns are related to lengths of sides and angles*
❖ *Shapes are conserved through flips and rotations*
❖ *Shapes are categorized and named depending on their properties*

❖ *Pathways have direction and distance*

Both rats and toddlers are able to reorient themselves using the borders of a space they have navigated previously (Cheng and Gallistel, 1984; Lee and Spelke, 2008). For example, if a toy is placed in a corner of a rectangular room that a 4 year-old has explored, and the toy is then removed, the child will return to the corners that exhibit the same characteristics—apparently using length of the walls and direction to reorient. When the room is a square and the walls are painted different colors they do not differentiate; color is not used as a visual clue. Instead they search all four corners equally. They also search all four corners when a 2-D drawing (for example a rectangle) is placed on the floor. Evidently it is the borders— the extended surfaces or walls of the environment and turns—that are important, and these are analyzed by young children using an early (perhaps even innate) sense of distance and direction as they navigate their surroundings. Thus, as they make maps, distance and turns (perhaps an early precursor of Euclidean geometry and Cartesian-coordinate space) become understood as helpful attributes to depict.

❖ Pathways traveled can be represented as lines with landmarks

Lines are first understood by young children as marks they make on paper as they move the pencil or crayon to and fro. These marks are not necessarily straight, but are often curved as a result of their actions. Thus they have a temporal characteristic: they represent an action or movement of the hand across the paper, from start to finish. As they attempt to make maps of their environment, children also use lines to represent the paths traveled. The line represents their motion: where they started and ended. It is a *temporal* representation and is embellished usually with pictures of the landmarks they passed along the way.

❖ Pathways can enclose space

Another early big idea in mapmaking is the realization that the beginning and end of their pathways can connect at the same place, and if they do the interior space is enclosed. This is an early form of *topological geometry*—a geometry that does not deal with distance, angle, or straightness, but with the property of being enclosed, or bounded.

❖ The shape of the enclosed space and the pathway itself can be analyzed by properties such as distance and turns

In order to differentiate rectangles from other polygons, such as hexagons or triangles, and to recognize that there are various sizes of rectangles, children begin to focus on the number of lengths, their distance, and the number of "corners." They construct the idea that paths and the enclosed spaces they make (polygons) are made up of straight lines and direction. Their navigational maps take on turns (and the number of them) and the lengths of lines take on a sense of distance. At this point in development children can begin to relate these characteristics to small movable objects and polygons (such as pattern blocks) and can name the interior bounded space, although they often name it incorrectly because they have not as yet constructed angle measurement, nor a Cartesian coordinate system with which to explain parallel lines. So, for example, if a navigational path has 4 corners and 4 straight lines, it may be called and drawn as a rectangle even though the angles may not be 90 degrees and the lines may not be parallel. With small movable shapes however, children easily detect that a rhombus and a rectangle are different. It is best to introduce the correct vocabulary naturally. Shapes with 4 sides and 4 angles (corners) are quadrilaterals. A rectangle and rhombus are two different kinds of quadrilaterals. A square is a special rectangle, the one where the sides are all the same length.

❖ Distance and turns are related to lengths of sides and angles

As children begin to coordinate the representations and characteristics of the two core cognitive systems (mapping the environment and analyzing the characteristics of shapes) they develop a more encompassing way of structuring the information in both. A directional turn becomes understood as an angle (although children most often call it a corner), and distance traveled is understood as a measurable length of a side. Now the two systems are a cohesive whole and a foundation has been built for the later development of a Cartesian-coordinate system, measurement of angles as rotations, and in general, *Euclidean geometry*.

❖ *Shapes are conserved through flips and rotations*

Children need many experiences rotating and flipping shapes to ensure they are congruent. Often an isosceles triangle shown 45 degrees off center is seen as being different than the same triangle shown with the base parallel to the edge of table. Understanding that shapes are conserved through transformation (orientation: flips, rotations, and slides) is a precursor to the development of *transformational geometry*.

❖ *Shapes are categorized and named depending on their properties*

Early in development, children view figures holistically without analyzing their properties. According to van Hieles (1985), children at first identify prototypes of basic geometrical figures (triangle, circle, and square). These visual prototypes are then used to identify other similar shapes. A shape is a circle because it looks like a sun; a shape is a rectangle because it looks like a door or a box; and so on. A square often at first seems to be a different sort of shape than a rectangle, and a rhombus does not look like other parallelograms, so these shapes are classified completely separately in the child's mind. If a shape does not sufficiently resemble its prototype, the child may reject the classification. The idea that shapes can be classified and named by their properties (number of sides and angles), in contrast to what they look like, is a huge cognitive leap—one that enables the formation of a larger hierarchical inclusive structure: for example all 4-sided figures are quadrilaterals, so a rectangle is also a quadrilateral, and a square is the regular version of a rectangle (when all the sides are equal), etc.

STRATEGIES

As you work with the activities in this unit, you will notice that students will use many strategies to solve the problems that are posed to them. Here are some strategies to notice:

- ❖ *Analyzes shapes only as visual objects*
- ❖ *Uses borders to orient*
- ❖ *Draws a map temporally, as a line of movement with landmarks*
- ❖ *Draws and recognizes shapes topologically*
- ❖ *Encodes shapes of surface layouts traveled*
- ❖ *Draws, analyzes, and sorts shapes using Euclidean properties*
- ❖ *Physically rotates objects to prove congruency*
- ❖ *Mentally rotates objects to prove congruency*

❖ Analyzes shapes only as visual objects

Students at this level recognize figures only by their appearance. For example they may say that a square is only a square when shown in the traditional orientation. When rotated they call it a diamond because it looks like a different shape to them (van Hiele, 1985).

❖ Uses borders of the environment traveled to orient

To determine where an object was seen, children use information from the boundary of the environment. For example, they might use the information of walking along a wall until getting to a corner and then turning and walking just a little farther, to locate something placed along the far wall near the first corner.

❖ Draws a map temporally, as a line of movement with landmarks

As they attempt to make maps of their environment, one of the earliest strategies children use is drawing a line to represent their motion in time: where they started and ended. The line is then embellished usually with pictures of the landmarks they passed along the way as a way to tell their "readers" what to look for.

❖ Draws and recognizes shapes topologically

Because children focus at first on enclosure and boundaries of the shape, rather than the Euclidean properties of length and angles, polygons are often all drawn the same. Children make no differentiation between a path that is rectangular, triangular, or circular, but they do know it is not linear. They also distinguish easily between closed and not-closed shapes: a donut is perceived as being different from a sphere, and three non-intersecting lines are perceived as being different from a triangle, but a triangle is considered similar to a rectangle or circle because only enclosure, boundaries, and openings are considered (Piaget, 1967).

❖ Encodes shapes of surface layouts traveled

As they listen to the read-aloud of the adventure of Baby, you will find some students able to encode the shape of the environment by using the information described. Four forward movements and four turns might be encoded as a rectangle (although the information is really only sufficient to call it a quadrilateral because the length of lines and angle measurements are unknown). Their maps show shapes, and the strategy of just drawing a timeline with landmarks is abandoned. Instead the distances and turns are shown.

❖ Draws, analyzes, and sorts shapes using Euclidean properties such as number of sides and angles (often called corners by children)

Polygons are now depicted as line segments and angles, rather than simply as bounded curved space, and shapes are sorted into categories by the same properties.

❖ Physically rotates objects to prove congruency

At first children are not able to determine if the shape would be the same if it was flipped or rotated. They need to physically move the object to check.

❖ Mentally rotates objects to prove congruency

Physical movement of the object to check for congruency is no longer needed. Children are able to mentally rotate or flip to establish congruency.

MATHEMATICAL MODELING

Initially models grow out of representing a situation (Gravemeijer, 1999). In this unit children engage in mapmaking as well as exploring of small movable objects and naming them. This unit attempts to foster coordination between the forms of representing navigational pathways and the drawings of 2-D and 3-D shapes to build a foundation for the development of Euclidean geometry (using line segments and angles), which demands an understanding and coordination of the attributes of length, distance, angle, and direction.

❖ Representing navigation (pathways)

Initially models grow out of visually representing the situation. In this unit navigation is used to generate maps depicting distance (length) and turns (angles).

❖ 2-D shapes

The unit is designed to encourage children to represent, sort, classify, and name 2-D shapes (on a plane) by representing them by their Euclidean properties (such as the number of sides and angles).

❖ 3-D shapes

The faces of the solids form 2-D shapes. As children explore 3-D solids in this unit, the properties of 2-D shapes (edges, corners) as well as polygons and vertices are used to describe, sort, and discuss relationships.

A graphic of the full landscape of learning for this unit is provided on page four. The purpose of the graphic is to allow you to see the longer journey of students' geometric development and to place your work with this unit within the scope of this long-term development. You may also find the graphic helpful as a way to record the progress of individual students for yourself. Each landmark can be shaded in as you find evidence in a student's work and in what the student says—evidence that a landmark strategy, big idea, or way of modeling has been constructed. In a sense, you will be recording the individual pathways your students take as they develop as young mathematicians.

References and Resources

Davies, Clare and David H. Uttal, 2007. Map use and the development of spatial cognition. In Jodie M. Plumert and John P. Spencer (eds.) *The Emerging Spatial Mind.* NY: Oxford University Press. pp. 219-247.

Dehaene, Stanislaus, Veronique Izard, Pierre Pica, and Elizabeth Spelke, 2006. Core knowledge of geometry in an Amazonian indigene group. *Science*. 311: 381-384.

Gravemeijer, Koeno P. E. 1999. How emergent models may foster the constitution of formal mathematics. *Mathematical Thinking and Learning 1* (2): 155–77.

Piaget, Jean and Barbel Inhelder. 1967. *The Child's Conception of Space*. New York: Norton.

Spelke, Elizabeth, Sang Ah Lee, and Veronique Izard. 2010. Beyond core knowledge: Natural geometry. *Cognitive Science*. May 1: 34 (5): 863-884.

van Hiele, Pierre. 1985 [1959]. *The Child's Thought and Geometry*, Brooklyn, NY: City University of New York, pp. 243–252.

DAY ONE

BEGINNING THE ADVENTURE

Materials Needed

Baby's Wild Adventure (Read-aloud Big Book or use Appendix A)

Blank sheets of paper

Writing Utensils

Clipboards (optional)

Baby and Blankie Cut-Outs (Appendix B)

Actual Baby Blanket (optional)

The context of baby's wild adventure is introduced to support the development of several big ideas and strategies related to geometry and measurement. The big book, *Baby's Wild Adventure*, is used to introduce students to the context—Baby is exploring the "wild outdoors" (the backyard) with her favorite "Blankie" (blanket). While exploring, Baby drops Blankie to get a closer look at the animals she encounters. As she crawls a distance, turns a corner, crawls some more and turns more corners, Baby surprisingly happens upon Blankie again!

After listening to the story, students attempt to solve the mystery…how does Baby keep finding Blankie when moving around and making turns? Using a blank piece of paper, students work to draw a map of Baby's adventure as they try to solve the blankie mystery. Through drawing and conferring with one another, students begin to explore and coordinate two core geometries: navigation and properties of two-dimensional shapes.

Day One Outline

Developing the Context
❖ Read *Baby's Wild Adventure* aloud.

❖ Ask students to work independently or in pairs to solve the blankie mystery by making drawings (maps) of the path Baby might have traveled.

Supporting the Investigation
❖ Note students' strategies as they draw their maps and elicit and discuss their different explanations for how Baby finds Blankie.

Developing the Context

Start by reading *Baby's Wild Adventure* (Available from Amazon.com in color, or use the black and white version provided as Appendix A), **but STOP before showing the map of the backyard at the end. DO NOT LET STUDENTS SEE THE MAP OF BABY'S BACKYARD.** After reading the story have students discuss the "blankie mystery" with a quick partner share. How could Baby keep finding Blankie? What might Baby's path have been?

Pair students together, but give *each* student a blank piece of paper and crayons or markers and ask them to discuss and draw the path Baby might have traveled. If you want you can provide each student with a clipboard to work on as well, but this is optional.

Teacher Note

There is not one expected answer or representation. Although enclosure of a shape is required for Baby to pass the same point twice and find Blankie, and this idea is at the heart of what we want the students to eventually construct, it is more important that students think and continue to puzzle over and solve the blankie mystery themselves than for you to lead them to a solution. Thus, you should not have students model the story all together while you read the story out loud, and DO NOT LET THEM SEE THE MAP OF THE BACKYARD AT THE END OF THE STORY. The map will be shown much later in the week.

Supporting the Investigation

As students work, move around the room and confer as needed to support and challenge their investigation. Some students may be so interested in the recalling and sequencing of the storyline that they forget to think about why Baby kept finding Blankie. Encourage these students to use the details of the story to help them figure out the blankie mystery. Prompting students to draw a map of where they think Baby traveled will encourage students to think about the various pathways Baby took on her adventure.

Differentiating Instruction

As students share their thinking encourage them to question one another and think about multiple possible solutions. You might ask, "Does that explanation prove how Baby found Blankie each time? How did she get back to Blankie?" Or, "Can more than one explanation work? Why or why not?" Use what you know about individual students to match them with an appropriate partner. To further support the conversation you may wish to:

- ❖ Provide each partnership with Baby and Blankie cut-outs (Appendix B). Using these manipulatives, partnerships can act out different parts of the story to work out their thinking.
- ❖ Gather a small group of students and re-read a portion of the story. As you re-read, partners can act out what they think is happening with the baby and blankie cut-outs, or use a real blanket and

physically crawl. Letting them puzzle is important, so do not try to direct the role-playing to get them to *your* solution. **The point of the role-playing should be *only* to foster discussion on the issues at hand and observe individual student development along the landscape of learning, not to lead everyone to the same solution.**

❖ Some children prefer to just draw a map of the situation right away and that is fine, too. Modeling the situation is a great way to start. Provide lots of paper so that they can make revisions as they work out their thinking.

As you walk around the room, you will notice students thinking about the problem in a variety of ways and your conferring should both celebrate what they are trying to do and challenge them to form new insights in relation to the landscape of learning in the Unit Overview. Some examples of student work that you might see are shown in Figures 1-3.

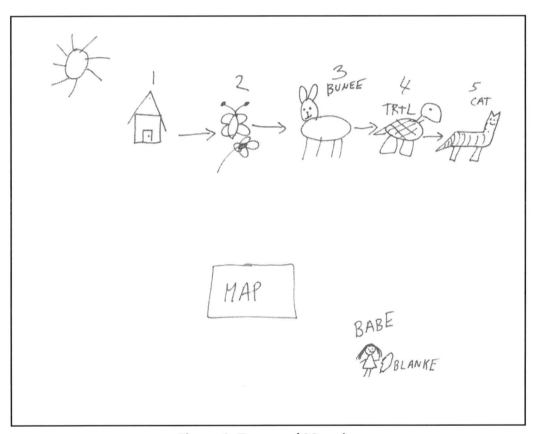

Figure 1: Temporal Mapping

Temporal Mapping: Several students will likely just list or draw the places Baby visited in a time sequence, often shown as a line. Their sequencing may even be out of order and they may only have a drawn a few of the places, forgetting to include others. Some students may list words to show the time sequence (such as flowers, vegetables, lake, building); others may sketch the places (see Figure 1) and use arrows or numbers to highlight where Baby traveled first, second, etc. However, in these drawings, the student does not draw the pathway that Baby crawled and has yet to construct the idea that the interior space formed as Baby moves around the objects is enclosed. Encourage these students to think about the blankie mystery. For example you might say, "Baby did visit all of those places. Where did she drop Blankie? Maybe you want to add that to your map. Then somehow Baby found Blankie again! That's interesting…How could she have come to it again?"

You may also choose to read a short passage detailing the crawling and turns that Baby took to find Blankie and encourage these students to draw a picture of this as well.

A Note About Magical Thinking

Many of the youngest students will be so taken by the narrative of the story that their solution to the blankie mystery will involve magical thinking. These students may think that the animals or the wind moved Blankie or that Mama was following Baby around with Blankie and dropped it for her to find again. Instead of discouraging this type of thinking, turn the discussion back to the students, "What do you think? Could this be an explanation for how Baby finds her blankie every time? Are there other possible reasons?" Have partnerships explore all possibilities. Many students can understand that Baby could travel all the way around an object and find Blankie again while also still believing that the yellow toad hopped around with Blankie in his mouth! Kindergarten is a golden age for magical thinking and it will only be the construction of the big idea about turns producing a closed, bounded space that will allow them to see how it could have happened logically. Discussion on the turns and the path Baby made supports this construction.

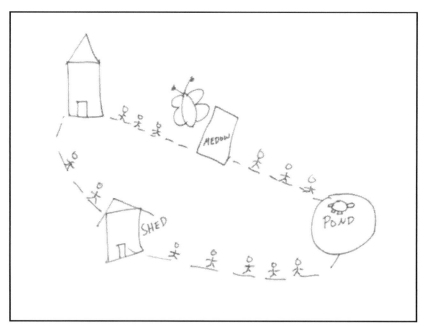

Figure 2: Topological Mapping

Topological Mapping: Other students will have an understanding that Baby traveled a pathway that ended where it began and will include some closed figures on their map, showing a beginning understanding that Baby had to travel all the way around the object and then found Blankie in the same place she dropped it! Many of these students intuitively understand that Baby traveled all the way around the lake and can show with their finger how Baby moved around in a circle. These students are more hesitant with the other places that Baby visited and may also draw the flower garden, vegetable garden, and cabin as circles or other shapes with curved lines instead of straight lines with turns forming corners (angles) and may not use the terminology 'turns', while explaining how Baby traveled. They understand the pathway to be around a closed figure, but not yet as one exhibiting the properties of line segments and angles. Encourage these students to share their thinking with their peers about how Baby found Blankie at the lake by going *all the way around the lake,* "How interesting! Do you think that is how Baby found Blankie every time, by going all the way around? Would that work at the flower garden, and the vegetable garden?" You may also choose to read a short passage detailing the crawling and turns that Baby took to find Blankie and encourage these students to refine their maps.

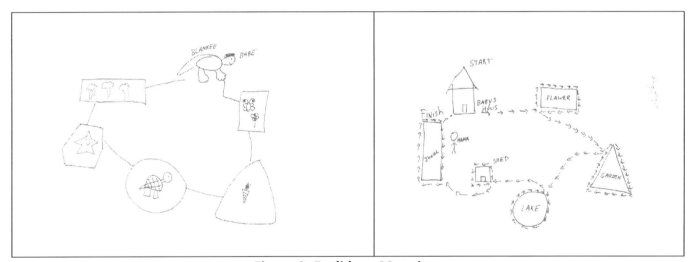

Figure 3: Euclidean Mapping

Mapping Making Use of Euclidean Properties: Some students will have a clearly drawn map of all the places that Baby visited using closed shapes with straight lines and well-defined turns (which they often call corners). The maps will be accurately drawn with quadrilaterals to represent the flower garden, jungle, and cabin, a triangle to represent the vegetable garden, and a circle to represent the lake. These students can clearly explain how Baby finds Blankie because she just goes all the way around each shape and finds Blankie right where she left it! In fact, many of these students will draw the pathway that Baby traveled as a series of dotted lines or arrows to prove how Baby travels all the way around. For these students, encourage them to think about how Baby turns, "Does it matter which way Baby turns? You went this way and then turned a corner to the left. Could Baby have turned to the right? How did we end up with a quadrilateral (4 sides and 4 turns)? How did that happen? Will it always happen?"

As you confer with students who do make Euclidean maps, you may find that they all draw rectangles or squares and that they argue about whether it is a rectangle or a square that Baby traveled around. This is an opportunity to revisit the book and discuss what is known from the story. Since all that is known is that Baby went forward four times and turned four times the shape could be drawn in several ways. However, they will all be quadrilaterals and this is a nice place to introduce the term and to engage children in a discussion on its properties. A rectangle is a quadrilateral with right angles, as is a square. A square is a special rectangle where all the lengths of the sides are the same. When the map of the backyard is revealed later in the week, children will see that the paths around the flower garden (meadow), the cabin (shed), and the jungle were all rectangles. The lake (small pond) was a circle, and the vegetable garden was a triangle.

Reflections on the Day

Students explored several big ideas about properties of two-dimensional shapes and direction today as they discussed the Blankie mystery and created their maps. Students were deepening their understanding of mapping and direction and coordinating these with the properties of two-dimensional shapes. You were able to witness the variety of strategies and to see which children are still only thinking temporally, while others are considering the ideas that shapes are enclosed, bounded areas (topological). Still others could describe the paths and turns with properties such as lines and corners (Euclidean). The context investigated today is a powerful one for constructing the idea that Baby may have traveled all the way around objects and her path created various shapes. On Day Two, students will continue with this work and a math congress will provide an opportunity for growth by discussing a few of their solutions to the Blankie mystery.

DAY TWO

SOLVING THE BLANKIE MYSTERY

Materials Needed

Baby's Wild Adventure (or use Appendix A)

Student Maps from Day One

Blank Sheets of Paper

Writing Utensils

Baby and Blankie Cut-Outs (Appendix B)

Document camera to project student maps (or take a photo with an iPad or cell phone and project it from a computer)

Actual Baby Blanket (optional)

Students return to work to review their maps and discuss with their partners from Day One how they solved the mystery of Baby's blanket. The purpose of revisiting this context is to allow for reflection and revision to student's previous drafts. This process supports growth and development. After they reflect and revise their work, students will discuss their work in a math congress.

Day Two Outline

Preparing for the Math Congress

❖ Provide students with time to review and revise their maps from the day before.

❖ Observe as they work, continuing to confer where helpful, and determine who will share during the math congress.

Facilitating the Math Congress

❖ Invite a few pairs of students to present to the class, highlighting on their own maps how Baby kept finding Blankie.

❖ Facilitate a conversation on a few of the big ideas on the landscape as pairs share.

Preparing for the Math Congress

Remind students of the story of *Baby's Wild Adventure* and their investigation on Day One. Have students review their maps with their partner from Day One and reflect on all the different possible solutions they thought of for why Baby continued to find Blankie. Have blank pieces of paper available in case students want to create new maps. Ask students to reflect on the following questions:

- ❖ How did Baby find Blankie?
- ❖ Did you think of more than one possible solution? Which one do you think is most likely?
- ❖ Where did Baby travel? What does the pathway look like?

Tips for Structuring the Math Congress

As students prepare, think about how you could structure the math congress to support everyone's development, even though students may be at very different places on the landscape of learning. This will likely mean focusing the discussion on students' reasoning and ideas, rather than students simply showing each other their products. To determine which students will share during the congress, observe them carefully with an eye to the landscape as they work and look for those who:

- ❖ Still hold onto magical thinking (believe the animals, wind, mom, or something else moved Blankie), with maps that attempt to show the time sequence.
- ❖ Understand that Baby went all the way around the lake and found Blankie right where she dropped it, but are not certain that Baby crawled all the way around the other shapes in a similar manner (emergent topological maps).
- ❖ Have maps that show Baby traveling all the way around each shape and attempt (or perhaps even accurately draw) two-dimensional shapes as closed figures with straight lines and corners (Euclidean maps).

Facilitating the Math Congress

Convene students in the meeting area and have a document camera available where you can show student maps. Have students sit next to their partners with their maps.

Tech Tip

You could take pictures of students' maps using an iPad and project them onto a whiteboard or smartboard. When different ideas come up in discussions, you can draw revisions without having to mark on the students' work. Apps such as *Adobe Sketch* or *Explain Everything* can be useful tools for this task.

You might begin by having the students with the magical thinking ideas share. Have the group discuss why or why these might not be possibilities **(Let the students discuss as a group and come to a consensus. The group may decide that those ideas could never work but it is more likely that the group will decide that it is a possibility but there are better explanations. Remember, students can understand that Baby turned corners and went all the way around objects while also still holding onto some magical thinking.)**

Next have a pair share that made a topological map. You might have them act out with Baby and Blankie cut-outs how Baby found Blankie. Ask other students if they agree and have them come up to show their understanding of their peers' work. Promote a discussion on what happened when Baby turned the corners.

At this time, you may also have some students act out portions of the story. Read a portion of the story while a student acts out dropping Blankie, crawling forward and turning corners until they happen upon Blankie again! Have a discussion on whether it matters which direction Baby turns.

Inside One Classroom: A Portion of the Congress

Alci: I think that the animals carried Blankie. Like the butterfly by the garden…

Kacey: The butterfly could not carry Blankie. It would be too heavy.

Alci: But the toad could. And the turtle.

Asha: I think the baby just kept going around.

Melanie (the teacher): Hmm. I'm not sure I understand, Asha.

Asha: I don't think it was the turtle. I think Baby kept crawling around the pond *(draws circle on the rug with her finger)* and found Blankie.

Melanie: I think I understand your idea but I'm not quite sure. Does anyone else think they can explain Asha's thinking?

Several students put thumbs on their knees to show they can paraphrase.

Author's notes

Melanie begins the congress by allowing ample time for a discussion on magical ideas. Her first move is simply to encourage children to offer other more logical explanations as a way to provide reflection on other possibilities.

Melanie has a very good idea about what Asha is thinking, and that is precisely why she has called on her, but by asking other children to consider Asha's idea Melanie creates a community of discourse.

Owen: It's like she said. Baby dropped Blankie *(puts both index fingers down)* and then kept crawling all around the pond *(draws circle on rug with one finger, bringing it back to meet the other)* and found Blankie again. **Sophie:** I think that is what happened at the garden too. **Melanie:** Hmm. Turn and talk to your neighbor about Sophie's idea. Could Asha's conjecture about the pond work on the other parts of the backyard as well?	*Melanie has succeeded in getting the children to consider an argument about topological ideas. The beginning and endpoint of the pathway traveled may be at the same place!!* *Pair talk is critical at this juncture as a big idea has just been put forth. Pair talk now will foster further reflection.*

Reflections on the Day

Today, students had the opportunity to reflect on their thinking, modify their maps, and entertain a variety of ideas. Most likely students are describing objects and shapes using terms such as "around," "next to," "above," and "beside" and have begun exploring properties of two-dimensional shapes as a series of forward movements and turns. In the math congress, they were encouraged to consider and evaluate several possible solutions to the blankie mystery. At this point there is still likely a range of development, but in the next few days students will continue to explore each of the places Baby visited in more depth with discussions on the shapes. Games will be introduced that further develop their understanding of two-dimensional shapes and by the second week of the unit they will begin classifying shapes using a variety of attributes.

DAY THREE

WHAT SHAPE IS THE MEADOW?

Materials Needed

Baby's Wild Adventure (or use Appendix A)

Student Maps from Days One and Two

Large Chart Paper for Posters

Markers

Baby and Blankie Cut-Outs (Appendix B)

Several copies of Footprint Cut-Outs per pair of students (Appendix C)

Glue sticks and scissors for each pair of students

Sticky Notes for Gallery Walk

Actual Baby Blanket (optional)

Students work in small groups to review the first section of Baby's Wild Adventure, where Baby visits the meadow with the beautiful flowers and sees a butterfly. Using large chart paper, the groups will make posters to defend their thinking and depict the shape that Baby traveled around. The posters will be placed around the room for a whole class "gallery walk".

Day Three Outline

Developing the Context
❖ Review the meadow section of the story with students by rereading that section aloud.

❖ Assist groups as they create posters showing what shape they believe the meadow is (what shape Baby traveled as she went around it).

Supporting the Investigation
❖ Confer with students as they work.

Facilitating the Gallery Walk
❖ Conduct a gallery walk to allow students time to reflect and com-ment on each other's posters.

Developing the Context

Remind students of the *Baby's Wild Adventure* story and their investigation on Day One and the ideas that came up in the congress on Day Two. Tell students that today they are going to further explore the idea that Baby traveled all the way around each shape to find Blankie.

> *If Baby had indeed traveled all around the meadow and thus came upon Blankie right where she had dropped it, what shape would the meadow be?*

Reread that section of the story noting how Baby went along 4 straight paths and turned 4 corners.

Let students know that when mathematicians have an interesting idea, they create posters that they give to other mathematicians to read. Their math writing gets published just like writers when they write books. Today students will have an important job of proving their thinking to the rest of their classmates by making posters. Divide your class into three or four groups and have them work together to figure out a way to represent their thinking on a large piece of chart paper using the cut-outs of the footprints (Appendix C). [Note: If you have a teacher's aide and/or a student teacher, you can each take a group and facilitate the discussion. If you have a large class and you are alone, you may find the management of these groups difficult. If so, it is fine to make several smaller groups, as it is often difficult for children at this age to collaborate in large groups without assistance from an adult.]

Supporting the Investigation

As groups work, move around the room and confer as needed. To support the groups you can:

❖ Have the group physically act out their portion of the story using a real blanket and crawling just like Baby did in the story. Encourage the group to think of ways that they can show this on their poster through drawing and writing.

❖ Give each group a baby and blankie cut-out.

❖ Provide each group footprint cut-outs that they can use to glue onto their poster to show how Baby moved around the shape.

❖ Once they have made their shape, students can color it to show the flowers and butterfly if they wish.

Facilitating the Gallery Walk

As groups finish, have them put their posters up in the classroom for other groups to view.

Once all of the groups have completed their posters, make sure all posters are placed around the room. Explain to your students that during a gallery walk they will walk around and look at the other posters. They will have an important job to think about: can they understand what another group was showing on their poster? Explain to students that they will walk silently around looking at the posters. As they walk around they should be thinking, "Do I understand this?" "Is this similar to what I did on my map or poster?" "Do I agree?" "Am I confused about a part?" "Do I disagree?"

Give your students sticky notes so that they can share their reactions to each poster. You may wish to give your students blank post-it notes so that they can draw/write their ideas or you may wish to provide them with the following pre-made sticky notes:

✓ **Check Mark:** I really understand this

? **Question Mark:** I wonder about this, or I have a question here

⇄ **Connection sign:** I agree. I did the same thing on my poster.

Give students only a few sticky notes so they have to think carefully about where they will place them.

Have students walk around the posters silently for 5-10 minutes. After the gallery walk, you can invite the groups to go back to their posters to see what comments were left for them. By having this gallery walk, you are encouraging your students to reflect and comment on written and visual forms of mathematics—something professional mathematicians do!

Reflections on the Day

Today, students had the opportunity to work in groups to clarify and represent their thinking through writing and drawing. Students had the chance to review other posters and think about whether they could understand what another group was defending. As students prepared their posters and participated in the gallery walk, they further explored properties of two-dimensional shapes as distances and turns. Tomorrow students will work in small groups to clarify and represent the remaining shapes that Baby traveled around in her backyard. As you think about each of your children, have you seen any growth along the landscape over the past few days?

DAY FOUR

REPRESENTING THE REMAINING BACKYARD SHAPES

Materials Needed

Baby's Wild Adventure (or use Appendix A)

Student Maps from Days One and Two

Large Chart Paper for Posters

Markers

Baby and Blankie Cut-Outs (Appendix B)

Several copies of Footprint Cut-outs (Appendix C)

Glue stick and scissors for each group of students

Places Baby Went (Appendix D)

Sticky Notes for Gallery Walk

Actual Baby Blanket (optional)

Students work in small groups to review the remaining sections of *Baby's Wild Adventure*. Today each of eight groups will look at a section of the story and make posters to defend their thinking, as they all did with the meadow on Day Three. The posters will again be placed around the room for a whole class "gallery walk." Afterwards the map of Baby's Backyard, provided on the last page of the read aloud (or of Appendix A), will be examined and discussed by the class as a whole.

Day Four Outline

Developing the Context
❖ Reread the book and then give a section of the story (cut from Appendix D) to each of eight groups, providing two groups each with the same section.

Supporting the Investigation
❖ Assist groups as they create the shape of each place that Baby traveled around.

Facilitating the Gallery Walk
❖ Conduct a gallery walk to allow students time to reflect and comment on each other's posters.

Facilitating the Math Congress
❖ Convene a meeting to examine the map provided at the end of the read-aloud (book or Appendix A).

Developing the Context

Reread the story and review the posters made on Day Three. You may wish to engage your students in a discussion on what information was most helpful to include on their meadow posters. Today they will again have the important job of proving their thinking to the rest of their classmates by making posters of the remaining areas that Baby traveled.

Divide your class into eight groups and ask them to work together to figure out the shape of the vegetable garden, the lake, the cabin, and the jungle. It is best to have at least two groups working on each of the four sections. As groups finish they can check with the other group that worked on the same section to see if they agree. If groups finish earlier than others and want to do more than one section they can. By working on a second poster, students have further opportunities to coordinate the two geometries of navigation and shapes, and to consider how best to represent their mathematical ideas clearly and concisely for their audience.

Supporting the Investigation

As groups work, move around the room and confer as needed. To support the groups you can:

❖ Have the group physically act out their portion of the story using a real blanket and crawling just like Baby did in the story. Encourage the group to think of ways that they can show this on their poster through drawing and writing.

❖ Give each group Baby and Blankie cut-outs to role play with if needed.

❖ Provide each group footprint cut-outs (Appendix C) that they can use to glue onto their poster to show how Baby moved around the shape.

Facilitating the Gallery Walk

As groups finish, have them put their poster up in the classroom for other groups to view.

Once all of the groups have completed their posters, make sure all posters are placed around the room. Students again will walk around the Gallery silently and post sticky-notes on the posters. As on Day Three you can use blank sticky-notes or pre-made ones. After the gallery walk, invite the groups to go back to their posters to see what comments were left for them.

Facilitating the Math Congress

Gather the students together with all of the posters visible. Do students agree that these are the shapes that Baby traveled in the backyard? Is another shape possible? Were some shapes easier to determine than others? Are any similar? If so, how?

After the discussion, reveal the map of Baby's Backyard at the end of the book.

Inside One Classroom: A Portion of the Congress

Pablo: The jungle is just like the cabin! 4 sides and 4 turns. It's a rectangle.

Kacey: It could be a square.

Melanie (the teacher): Could they both be right? Turn to your neighbor and discuss this.

Pablo: They both have 4 sides and 4 turns.

Tanika: The rectangle is long and skinny though.

Melanie: Hmm. Rectangles have 4 sides and 4 turns. So actually, a square is a rectangle too! But it is a very special one. What do you think makes it special?

Tanika: When you draw the square all the lines have to be the same.

Melanie: I think I understand your idea, Tanika. The square is a special kind of rectangle, isn't it? It's a rectangle that has 4 sides the same, so Baby would have had to crawl the same distance on every straight path for the jungle and cabin to be a square. Do we know if she did? *(Several students murmur that they don't know because it didn't say in the story.)* I think there is a map on the last page of the book. Shall we look at it and see if our predictions were right? *(Melanie shows the map of Baby's backyard, the last page of the read-aloud or Appendix A.)*

Owen: Hey, wow! *(Many students are gasping in surprise.)* It's like we said! The meadow was a rectangle! And the jungle was a rectangle!

Author's notes

Melanie focuses discussion here on a big idea. All that is known is that Baby went on 4 straight paths and took 4 turns. The shape is definitely a quadrilateral but it could be a rectangle or a square, too. This conversation pushes students to consider the properties of the shapes: the side lengths and the angles. Tanika's response is evidence that Melanie's question was powerful.

Although Tanika may still have been thinking about rectangles and squares being unrelated, Melanie continues to help her focus on both the similarities and the differences.

Melanie very naturally segues into a look at the map of the backyard.

Sophie: But the path around the cabin was a square, and it wasn't really a cabin. It was just a small shed! And the lake was a circle, but it really wasn't a lake….just a small pond!	*Melanie uses correct language naturally throughout the discussion and children easily pick it up.*
Melanie: Hmm. Turn and talk to your neighbor about this. Why did everything seem so big to Baby? Was she just in her own backyard all of the time?	*Pair talk is used again when reflection can be helpful. Another big idea related to scale is at play here.*
(At this point most of the children are surprised and delighted to see that everything seems so large to Baby because she is so small and she was safe in her backyard the whole time.)	

Reflections on the Day

Today, students had another opportunity to work on developing their mathematical thinking and reasoning. As a group, they figured out the possible shapes that Baby traveled and then the map of Baby's backyard was revealed. Over the next several days, students will play games that further develop their understanding of two-dimensional shapes and they will begin classifying shapes using a variety of attributes.

DAY FIVE

PLAYING IN BABY'S BACKYARD

Materials Needed

Baby's Wild Adventure
(or use Appendix A)

Map of Baby's Backyard (last page of Appendix A)

Location Cards
(Appendix E)

Baby and Blankie Cut-Outs
(Appendix B)

Writing utensils

Paper

Clipboards (optional)

Yesterday the map of Baby's Backyard was revealed. Today students will be given their own copy of the map and, using cut-outs of Baby and Blankie, they work on giving directions to help Baby find her lost Blankie and get home. In this activity, children will work on using positional language (e.g. next to, behind, on the side of, at the corner of) and the vocabulary of turns and straight paths as they continue to explore and navigate around two-dimensional shapes.

Day Five Outline

Developing the Context

❖ Provide copies of the map of Baby's Backyard and model how to play in Baby's Backyard: giving Baby directions to help find her Blankie and take it home.

Supporting the Investigation

❖ Note children's strategies and language as they give directions and confer as they work.

Facilitating the Math Congress

❖ Pairs of children will share their directions on how Baby found her missing Blankie and took it home.

Developing the Context

Gather the children around you and tell them that today they will get a chance to play in Baby's Backyard. Using their own copy of the map and cut-outs of Baby and Blankie, they will give Baby directions to get Blankie and go home. To introduce the investigation it is helpful to model how to play it first.

Directions: Students work in pairs. One student picks a location card and places Baby at that location. The other student selects another location card and places Blankie in that location. Students then give and/or write directions for Baby to get Blankie and go home. If writing is difficult, you may wish to take an oral dictation or pair that student with a stronger writer. If most of your children will have difficulty writing (even using invented spelling) you can keep this activity verbal, or you can use dice and have them play it as a board game.

Supporting the Investigation

Things to look for as you confer with students: Are students able to place Baby and Blankie using the positional language on the location cards? Do they know what the words mean? If not, this is an important time for you to help them understand positional language.

Some students may still give directions using landmarks, evidence that they are still challenged by the idea that pathways can enclose space and be described by distances and turns. Note where these ideas are on the landscape provided in the Overview and support children to begin to use these properties. For example, some children might say, "go to the pond to get Blankie and then go to the cabin and then go by the jungle." As you confer, support them to use forward steps and turns instead.

Are students giving the most concise directions for Baby to find Blankie? Are they looking for the fastest, most efficient way to get Blankie and go home? If not, support them to consider other pathways, reminding them that mathematicians always like to find fast, efficient ways to solve problems.

Preparing for the Math Congress

As you circulate among the students as they give directions, think about how you could structure the math congress to support everyone's development. You may see:

- ❖ Students relying primarily on positional language to give directions
- ❖ Students who are missing steps in their directions (for example turns)
- ❖ Students using both positional language and the language of turns and paths
- ❖ Students who get Baby home but in circuitous, non-efficient ways

It is helpful to think ahead about what ideas you want the congress to be on. Take a look again at the landscape. Given what you have noticed the children doing, are there ideas on the landscape you can focus on in a discussion?

Facilitating the Math Congress

For the congress you can project the map of Baby's Backyard onto a smart board, or you can make ahead a larger scale version of the Backyard and lay it out in the middle of a circle.

Invite a few partnerships to share their directions with the whole class, placing Baby and Blankie to match their starting points. The class can help refine any pieces of the directions that may be confusing or missing. Rich discussion among the children makes for a powerful learning environment, so let the children discuss options and offer suggestions. Don't be too quick to tell children what to do.

Find moments when they come up naturally to remind the children about the shapes that can form from pathways. For example if a pair gives directions around the cabin you might maximize the moment and have pair talk about the square that was just formed.

Reflections on the Day

Today, children wrote their own directions for traveling through Baby's Backyard. They had the opportunity to use, compare, and contrast this map to the one that they had envisioned earlier in the week. Using positional language and the vocabulary of turns and straight paths, children worked together to navigate the map and give directions for Baby to find Blankie and take it home. Tomorrow students will continue to use their knowledge of two-dimensional shapes as they begin to explore further and play games with two-dimensional shapes.

DAY SIX

SHAPE GAMES

Materials Needed

Quick Image Shapes
(Appendix F)

Shape Cards
(Appendix G, both sets
A and B)

Direction cards
(Appendix H)

**Geoboards and
elastics**

Quick images using shapes are introduced in a minilesson today to help students begin to attend to the attributes of shapes. Two games are then introduced, which further support children to analyze shapes based on their properties.

Day Six Outline

Minilesson: Quick Images
❖ Display a string of quick images using shapes. The shapes have been chosen to challenge children to analyze shapes by their properties, rather than by just a visual image.

Developing the Context
❖ Model how to play two new games: *Make a Shape* and *Shape Match*.

Supporting the Investigation
❖ Note children's strategies and language as they play the games and challenge them where appropriate.

Facilitating the Math Congress
❖ Students share strategies and/or big ideas that have emerged through playing the games.

Minilesson: Quick Images (10 – 15 minutes)

Using an enlarged cut-out version of the shapes from Appendix E, show image #1 for a few seconds and then remove it. Ask the children to consider the name and more importantly to describe the shape they saw to justify how they know it was that shape; then ask them to turn and tell their neighbor which shape they saw and how they knew it was that shape. Invite a few children to share their answers focusing the discussion on the number of sides and corners and then move to the next image. After you present image #4 and ask for answers, and while students are still looking at it, rotate the shape so that the sides are oriented vertically and horizontally. Solicit answers again, discussing how it is still a square no matter the orientation.

The string of shapes:

Image #1:

Image #2:

Behind the Crafting of the Minilesson

The string starts with an easily recognized shape in a common orientation. Image 2 is the same triangle, rotated 180 degrees. Students may call this a "cone" or an "upside-down triangle." A goal is to get them to see that it is the three corners that make it a triangle, not the orientation. Image 4 will also be presented in two different orientations to give students further opportunities to explore this idea.

Image #3:

Image #4:

Image #5:

Inside One Classroom: A Portion of the Minilesson

Susanna (the math coach) briefly shows image 1.

Susanna: What shape did you see? And, how do you know? Show with your thumbs when you are ready to respond. (*Waits until most thumbs are up*). Ok, turn and tell your neighbor. (*As students talk, Susanna moves around and listens to the reasoning.*) Logan?

Logan: It is a triangle.

Joseph: It has 3 sides.

Susanna: Let's look at it again. (*Susanna shows the image again.*) Is Joseph right? Does it have 3 sides? (*murmors of agreement*). Does it have any corners?

Alci: Yes, 3 corners.

Logan: That's how I knew it was a triangle. It has 3 sides and 3 corners.

Susanna briefly shows image 2:

Susanna: What shape did you see? And, how do you know?

Evan: It is a cone.

Lily: It is an upside-down triangle.

Susanna rotates image 2 so it is like the first image, modeling Lily's idea.

Lily: Wait (*tilting head to side*)...Now I don't know.

Susanna: Talk to your neighbor. Are these two shapes the same? (*Pauses, waits for thumbs.*) Who can say what their neighbor thinks about this?

Quinton: Hailey thinks they are the same shape-- they both have 3 sides and you just turned it.

Hailey: Quinton said that if it has 3 sides it is always a triangle.

Author's notes

By showing the image only briefly yet requesting that they explain how they know, Susanna is attempting to support her young mathematicians to focus on the properties of the shapes shown.

As is common at this age, some of the children do not analyze the shapes by their properties at first. Evan's response is evidence of this: he names it a cone because he sees it as a different visual image than the first.

By encouraging pair talk at this moment, Susanna provides time for reflection to resolve cognitive disequilibrium. By asking children to describe what their partners think, she also implicitly is stating that talk must be accountable—listening is as important as talking.

Susanna: What did you and Evan decide, Lily? **Lily**: It has 3 corners too. They both do. They are both triangles. **Evan**: Yep, it's a triangle, just an upside-down one.	*Susanna makes sure that she returns to Evan and Lily to see if there has been any cognitive reordering: are they now able to focus on the properties of the shapes?*

Developing the Context

Have students sit in a circle to learn the games. Choose a child to be your game partner as you model how to play.

Game #1: *Make a Shape*

Object of the game: The purpose of the game is to use the direction cards to make the corresponding shape on the geoboard.

Materials: Direction cards (Appendix H), 1 pack per pair of students; geoboards, 1 per student; and rubber bands

Directions: Student #1 flips over a card from the Direction Card pile. Each student uses a rubber band(s) to build the shape that would correspond to the specifications on the card. When they each have made the corresponding shape they share their boards with each other and check if all of the shapes match the card's directions. When they agree all of the shapes match the directions, they name the shape and clear their boards. Student #2 flips over a new card and they start again.

Things to look for as you confer with students: Do the students build the same type of shape (i.e. equilateral triangle with the point up) every time? Encourage them to consider if other triangles can be made and focus discussion on how there might be many ways to make a shape with 3 turns and 3 straight paths and they would all form triangles, even if they looked different!

Game #2: *Shape Match*

Object of the game: This game is played in groups (two to six players in a group). The purpose is to get as many pairs of same-shape cards as possible. This game is best played cooperatively as young children don't often understand the role of chance but we provide directions for a cooperative version and a competitive version so that you can choose.

Cooperative version: the pairs of cards get put into a joint pile and the goal is to get as many into that pile as possible. Players try to better their group score, counting the accumulated pairs and comparing the results of each round.

Competitive version: each player keeps an individual pile of pairs and results are compared at the end of the game. The player with the highest score wins.

Materials: Direction Cards (Appendix H); Shape Cards (Appendix G, both sets, A and B)

Directions: Both decks of cards are shuffled and mixed up together and then all of the cards are laid out face-up. Students take turns matching a direction card with a face card (for example, a student could choose a card with a triangle on it, then a direction card with 3 turns and 3 straight lines). The student shows the pair of cards to the others playing the game. If all agree that there is a match, the next player goes. Play continues until there are no more possible matches.

Challenge (played like Concentration): Lay some or all cards out face-down in a grid. Played competitively, Student #1 turns over two cards. Matches could be a shape card and a direction card, two matching shape cards (such as two triangles), or two identical direction cards. If the two cards are a match, the student keeps the pair and gets to go a second time. If she gets a match again she gets to keep those as well but the turn is over. If the cards don't match, the student puts them back and it is Student #2's turn. Played cooperatively, students again take turns, but they help each other remember where the cards are and they make as many matches together as they can.

Supporting the Investigation

Things to look for as you confer with students as they play *Make a Shape*: Do the students build the same type of shape (i.e. equilateral triangle with the point up) every time? Encourage them to consider if other triangles can be made and focus discussion on how there might be many ways to make a shape with 3 turns and 3 straight paths and that they would all form triangles, even if they looked different!

Things to look for as you confer with students as they play *Shape Match*: Are the students analyzing the shapes by focusing on properties, specifically seeing that the less commonly-shown varieties of triangles are still, technically, triangles? How are they deciding whether there is a match (counting corners, just looking and guessing, comparing with another card)? What language are they using to discuss whether or not there is indeed a match?

Inside One Classroom: Conferring

Susanna (math coach): (*conferring with 2 children, Evan and Lily, as they play Shape Match*) Are you arguing about whether these two shapes are the same?

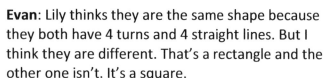

Evan: Lily thinks they are the same shape because they both have 4 turns and 4 straight lines. But I think they are different. That's a rectangle and the other one isn't. It's a square.

Susanna: Do you think you could both be right? (*The arguing stops as both consider the possibility that Susanna has put forth. Both students look very perplexed, however.*)

Evan: Rectangles are long and skinny. A square isn't.

Lily: But both shapes have 4 corners and 4 straight paths.

Susanna: I think you are both right. That is a rectangle and this one is a square. And they both have 4 sides and 4 corners. If Baby was following the path around the square, how would it be different than if she was following the path around this one (*pointing to the non-square rectangle*)?

Evan: She would have a long path and then a short one, and then a long one, and another short one. But, the straight parts on the square are all the same size.

Susanna: That's why you are both right. They are both rectangles because they have 4 turns like these (*points to the corners*) and 4 sides. But this one is a really special kind of rectangle and it has its own name: a square. The sides are all the same length. Baby would have to travel the same distance along each side, just like you said Evan.

Author's notes

Susanna begins the conferral by trying to understand the thinking of the children. Once she understands their thinking, she makes her first move. She tries to create disequilibrium with her question, "Could you both be right?"

Since both children adamantly stick to their reasoning, Susanna explains why she thinks they are both right. However she challenges further by asking them how the two shapes are similar and how they are different. She does this by asking them to imagine Baby in the story that was read on Day One.

Evan has now analyzed both shapes by describing the properties. The story context has even enabled him to begin considering length as a measureable attribute. Susanna can now provide the appropriate labels. Naming the shapes is social knowledge and so Susanna does not hold back in introducing the correct terminology. However she ensures that she does so only in the context of children first understanding.

Preparing for the Math Congress

As you circulate among the students as they play the games, think about how you could structure the math congress to support everyone's development. You may see:

❖ Students playing the *Make a Shape* game who made lots of different types or sizes of triangles while playing the game

❖ Students playing the *Shape Match* game who used an effective strategy to figure out whether or not there is a match

❖ Students who argued that shapes were different, even though the properties were the same

Facilitating the Math Congress

Convene students in the meeting area. Have students sit next to their partners and have a set of cards available from each game you wish to have conversation on.

Have students share an efficient strategy from one of the games, particularly a strategy that perhaps some other students were not yet using and could benefit from seeing (for example analyzing shapes by their properties). Do not feel that you need to find a strategy from each game. In fact, several good strategies from the same game could make for a very effective congress. For example, arguments such as the one depicted in the previous dialogue box (conferring) would make a powerful discussion.

Remember that it is important to set the expectation that all members of the community of mathematicians in the classroom participate by listening carefully and/or contributing verbally. Once a pair or group has shared, make sure to turn the conversation back to the whole group to reflect, perhaps through pair share and then reporting back or perhaps a survey: hand on your head if you used the same strategy; thumb up if you understand and want to try the strategy; hand in the air if you don't understand or have a question about the strategy.

Reflections on the Day

Today, students had the opportunity to explore further some of the big ideas and strategies they began to construct in the initial investigations of the backyard. The games allow them to continue to connect the properties of shapes with the idea of navigating around them. If possible, continue to make the games available during choice time or indoor recess in the following weeks to allow students to continue that work. You can even send sets of materials home and tell your students to teach their parents the new games!

DAY SEVEN

LEAVE A TRACK

Materials Needed

Direction Cards
(Appendix H)

Footprint Cutouts
(Appendix C)

Shape cards
(Appendix G, set A
only)

Writing utensils

Recording sheet
(Appendix I)

Tape or glue sticks

The game *I-Spy* is introduced in a minilesson today. This minilesson further supports children to analyze shapes by their properties. Afterwards, a new game is introduced: *Leave a Track*. Students play in pairs and then share their discoveries in math congress.

Day Seven Outline

Minilesson: *I-Spy*

❖ Play *I-Spy* with shape cards (set A only).

Developing the Context

❖ Model how to play the game *Leave a Track.*

Supporting the Investigation

❖ Note children's strategies and language as they play the game and challenge them further where appropriate.

Minilesson: *I-Spy* (10 – 15 minutes)

Materials: Shape cards (Appendix G, set A only)

Have the students sit around the circle and lay out the cards from Set A in the middle of the circle so that everyone may see. Alternatively, you can put the cards on a board with magnets, or project them onto a smart board.

Begin the game by giving a clue, such as "I spy, with my little eye, a shape that has four sides and four turns." Ask students to give a "thumbs-up" sign when they think they have a shape that fits the clue. As you call on students who have found a shape that fits, ask them to take the card from the center of the circle and place it in front of them. This can continue until all of the cards that can fit the clue have been picked up. If there are still cards that fit the clue in the center, you can say, "I spy another, I think." It is fun to do this even when there are none left that fit, because then the children have to prove you wrong! Once all the cards are removed give the students a few moments to pair share: looking at the cards that have been chosen, do they agree that they all fit the clue given? Call on a few students to justify the cards they chose based on the clue, then using the properties described provide the correct label (such as rectangles). For example, you might say, "I think we spied all of the rectangles!" Then have everyone put the shapes back in the center for a second round.

Minilesson:

- ❖ I spy, with my little eye, a shape that has 4 sides and 4 turns.
    - ○ (Children should identify all rectangles, including the squares)
- ❖ I spy, with my little eye, a shape that has 4 sides and 4 turns and all the sides are the same length.
    - ○ (Children should identify only squares)
- ❖ I spy, with my little eye, a shape that has 3 sides and 3 turns.
    - ○ (Children should identify all triangles)
- ❖ I spy, with my little eye, a shape that has 3 sides and 3 turns and all of the sides are the same length.
    - ○ (Children should identify only the equilateral triangle)

Inside One Classroom: A Portion of the Minilesson

(Susanna has previously given the clue that her shape has 4 sides and 4 turns. Students have selected all of the cards that fit that clue and have justified their choices.)

Susanna (math coach): I spy, with my little eye, a shape with 4 sides and 4 turns, but this time the sides are all the same length.

Nathaniel (interjecting): What do you mean?

Susanna: Remember when Baby went around the cabin? The sides were all the same. Baby went the same distance on every side before she got to the corner.

Alci: I know, I know! It's a square! I spy a big one and a little one!

Nathaniel: We had those out before. They are rectangles.

Susanna: You are right, Nathaniel. They are rectangles. But they are special ones because all of the sides are the same and so mathematicians give them a special name. They call them squares, too. It's like you and your brother are both Smiths. But if I say Nathaniel, it's only you. Which rectangles did we have to put back that weren't squares?

Author's notes

Class inclusion, the idea that squares are included in the group of rectangles, is very difficult for children to understand. However if Susanna always singled out the non-square rectangles and called only them the rectangles, children would erroneously come to believe the shapes were different. By using correct terminology, Susanna is encouraging her children to consider both similarities and differences and to understand that shapes are sorted by the properties of the number of sides and the number of angles (turns). She uses the example of first and last names as a way to help children understand the inclusion. Nathaniel Smith has two names because he is in the Smith family, but only he is Nathaniel.

Developing the Context

Have students sit in a circle to learn the game. Choose a child to be your game partner as you model how to play.

Game: *Leaving a Track*

Object of the game: The object of the game is to walk the outline of a closed shape (leaving a track of "footprints") following the directions given on the card but adding in a number of steps, and then to draw the shape on the recording sheet (Appendix I).

Materials: deck of direction cards (Appendix H, one set per pair), stack of cut out paper footprints (Appendix C), writing utensils, recording sheet (Appendix I), tape or glue sticks

Directions: Students choose who will give directions and who will walk and leave a track. The director pulls a direction card AND DOES NOT SHOW the card to the follower. The director gives directions to the follower on where to go and what to do. The follower leaves a paper footprint for every step he/she takes. When the shape is closed, the director shows the direction card to the follower and they decide if the footprint shape matches the direction card. Then they tape or glue the direction card to the recording sheet. Next, both students draw, on the recording sheet, the shape outlined by the footprints. They switch roles and try another card.

Inside One Classroom: Developing the Context (*Leave a Track*)	
Susanna (math coach) introduces the game, and then begins to model it with Lawrence.	
Susanna: I'm going to choose a direction card but I am not going to let Lawrence see it because he is going to follow my directions without knowing what the shape is going to be. But I will show all of you in case I need your help. (*Shows direction card around. It is 3 sides and 3 turns*). Lawrence, please take 4 steps forward. (*He does, leaving footprints as he walks*). Now turn.	*Author's notes*
	Susanna engages the whole class in learning how to play by inviting them in on her role. She shows them the direction card and invites them to help her.
Lawrence: (*Looks puzzled, then turns completely around--360°. Several students smile and hands go up right away.*)	

Susanna: I think I need your help already! What happened?	*Angles as a turn, a rotation, are being introduced here naturally as navigational directions.*
Katherine: He went all the way around! You need to tell him how much to turn. Tell him to turn a little bit.	
Lawrence: Like this? (*turns about 30°*)	
Sammy: Tell him where to look. Like 'turn to look at the door.'	
(*Lawrence turns to the door.*)	*This is an important idea that Sammy has suggested. Orientation matters. The turn is actually a new orientation.*
Susanna: What should our next direction be?	
Katherine: Walk 3 steps.	
(*Lawrence walks three steps, leaving footprints as he goes.*)	
Katherine: Now walk 5 steps.	
Sammy: Wait! You forgot the turn. Turn to the bookshelf.	
Katherine: Then walk 5 steps to where you started.	
Susanna: Did we do it?	*Katherine's statement of "back to where you started" shows evidence of an understanding of topological space. The shape is now enclosed.*
Lawrence: But I only made 2 turns.	
Susanna: How do we complete the shape?	
Katherine: He needs to turn at the end back to the beginning.	
Susanna: Lawrence, what do you think Katherine means?	
Lawrence: (*turning once more*) Like this, so I'm going like I was when I started. Hey, I made a triangle!	
Susanna: Does that match our direction card? Turn to your neighbor and check in with them.	*Children will often be surprised when they see the shape they have made.*

Supporting the Investigation

Things to look for as you circulate around the students: Are students able to follow directions from peers? Are the directors using accurate directions? What strategies are they using to direct how large the turn should be? Are they able to prove that the footprint shape matches the direction card? Are they able to translate the footprint shape into drawing? Do they draw a shape that approximates the footprint shape (taking into consideration the length of the sides) or just any shape with the same number of sides?

Reflections on the Day

Today, students had the opportunity to continue to construct and coordinate the relationships between the two core geometries of navigation and shapes. The attributes of distance and turns are being related to lengths of sides and angles. If possible, continue to make the games available during choice time or indoor recess to allow the students to continue that work. Over the next few days, students will revisit Baby's backyard and begin to explore 3-D shapes.

DAY EIGHT

3-D SHAPE GAMES

Students begin the work of the day with the introduction of some new shapes: 3-D solids. After discussing how the shapes in the map of Baby's backyard were flat and these new shapes are 3-D solids, a minilesson with Quick Images challenges the students to match 3-D shapes with a 2-D image from their faces. Then they are introduced to two new games that allow them to continue exploring the solids, encouraging students to attend to their properties.

Day Eight Outline

Minilesson: 3-D shape sort
❖ Display a string of quick images using faces from the 3D shapes.

Developing the Context
❖ Model how to play two new games: *Copy Cat* and *Are You Feeling it?*

Supporting the Investigation
❖ Note children's strategies and language as they play the games and challenge or support them where appropriate.

Facilitating the Math Congress
❖ Students share strategies and/or big ideas that have emerged through the playing of the games.

Minilesson: Quick Images with 3-D Shape Match (10 – 15 minutes)

Materials: a set of 3-D solids, paper cut-outs of each face of the set you use

Put a complete set of the 3-D solids out where all students can see them. Show one cutout (of one of the faces) for a few seconds as a quick image and then remove it. Ask students to think about which of the 3-D solids from the set would have a matching face; then ask them to turn and tell their neighbor which 3-D shape they think works and why they think so. Invite a few children to share their answers and check out their predictions by placing the solid appropriately on the cut-out. Then move to the next image. Make sure that when there is more than one possibility (for example, pyramid and triangular prism for the triangle; cube and rectangular prism for the square) that students have a chance to see both and compare.

Image #1

Image #2

Image #3

Image #4

Behind the Crafting of the Minilesson

The string starts with a square: an easily recognized shape in a common orientation. It can be the bottom, side, or top of the cube; the bottom of the square pyramid; or the side of the triangular prism, etc. Image 2 is the triangle, which can be a face on the square pyramid; the bottom of a triangular prism, etc. The matches will depend on the set of 3-D solids you use and the cut-outs you make. However the minilesson is designed to support children to start noticing the properties of the solids.

As you work through the minilesson it is important to discuss a variety of possible choices and focus discussion on the properties and attributes of shapes. The goal of the minilesson is to support children to start analyzing the solids by focusing on their faces.

Inside One Classroom: A Portion of the Minilesson

Susanna (math coach) briefly showing image 2.

Susanna: What shape did you see? And, what solid do you think might have it as a face? Show with your thumbs when you are ready to respond. (*Waits until most thumbs are up*). Ok, turn and tell your neighbor. (*As students talk Susanna moves around and listens to the reasoning.*) Dylan?

Dylan: It was a triangle. I see it on the side of this one. (*points to the square pyramid*)

Joseph: Yep. It has 4 of them!

Susanna: Let's check. (*Susanna shows the image again and lays the pyramid down on it showing that it matches.*) Is Joseph right, too? Does the square pyramid have 4 faces that are triangles? (*murmors of much agreement*).

Maia: This one has a triangle too (*pointing to the triangular prism*).

Susanna: Wow, that's great noticing, Maia. This one in fact is called the triangular prism! Let's look at it. It does have a triangle on the bottom and the top! Let's see if it matches the quick image shape.

Maia: Nope. That one is big and these are little and so only this one matches.

Susanna: But you are right; both have triangles! Do we see any other triangles as faces on other solids, even if they don't match the quick image?

Author's notes

By showing the image only briefly yet requesting that they consider which solids might have it as a face, Susanna is attempting to support her young mathematicians to focus on the properties of the shapes and solids shown.

Susanna maximizes moments in the conversation, commenting on what children offer to introduce vocabulary and highlight the math: "Does the square pyramid have 4 faces that are triangles?"

Susanna supports and acknowledges Maia for what she has noticed and then challenges the group to consider other solids that might have triangular faces. This move keeps the focus on analysis of the properties.

Developing the Context

Have students sit in a circle to learn the games. Choose a child to be your game partner as you model how to play. If you only have a few sets of 3-D shapes, have these games be one station and bring in the games from Days Six and Seven to be the other stations. (Or, if your school has purchased an account with www.DreamBox.com, you could have some of your children on computers as you introduce the games.) Rotate until all of the students have had a chance to try the new games.

Game: *Copy Cat*

Object of the game: The purpose of the game is to provide opportunities for students to use language to describe both shape and orientation.

Materials: Two sets of 3-D shapes for each pair of students; paper and writing utensils

Directions: Begin with a limited number of solids (three or four). Students begin by checking to make sure that each has the same limited and identical set of blocks. Students sit back-to-back so that neither can see the other's blocks. Student #1 chooses a block, describes the block, and then tells what he is doing with the block. ("I am standing this block on the square end," or "I am placing the cylinder on top of the cube.")

Student #2 attempts to follow the directions and do the same thing with her blocks.

When all the blocks are placed, the students move to see if they were able to construct the same thing. If there are differences, have the students try to figure out what happened and work together to make the structures identical. Then each student should draw the structure she made. Then the students switch roles.

Teacher Note

Do not give too much input as to the kind of directions that should be given – that feedback should come by seeing how successful (or not) the directions were. Students can continue to take turns with the different roles and discuss how to give better directions. More blocks can be made available for more complicated structures when you want to challenge students.

Game: *Are You Feelin' It?*

Object of the game: The purpose of this game is to provide students with opportunities to sort and analyze shapes and solids by their properties.

Materials: Each player has a non-transparent bag of 3-D solids (students should be able to place a hand in the bag easily).

Directions: The first step is for students to make sure that they have the exact same blocks in each bag. When they have confirmed that each bag contains the same solids, they should sit back-to-back so that neither can see the other's lap.

Student #1 reaches into his bag, pulls out a block, and describes it using clues, but NOT the name. For example, a student might say, "My block has 6 faces. All of the faces are the same."

Student #2 reaches into her bag and attempts to find the block being described. In this case, it might be the cube. When Student #2 thinks she has the correct shape, she and Student #1 turn to face each other and compare the shapes they are holding. The blocks stay out of the bag if they match. If not, they go back in the bags and students rotate. Student #2 now pulls one out and describes it. Play continues until the bags are empty.

Supporting the Investigation

As you move around, notice if students are using language that is specific enough to be helpful to the partner. Are they able to reflect on what went awry when the structures do not match? Are they able to translate the 3-D structure into a drawing? What strategies do they try?

Are the students using appropriate and accurate vocabulary as they describe the shapes? Are the listeners able to differentiate the shapes without looking? In cases where this is too challenging, you can have the students line up the shapes out of the bag and play that way instead.

Facilitating the Math Congress

Convene students in the meeting area. Have students sit next to their partners and have a set of 3-D shapes available for students who will need to refer to them as they share.

Have students think about a challenge they faced in one of the games, and how they faced that challenge. Give them a few minutes to ponder or whisper with their partner before inviting pairs to share with the whole group. Have a few students role-play a few of the strategies they tried, the challenges they met, and some of the solutions. Remind students that mathematicians work really hard trying to solve problems and they hate giving up. They even say, "When problems are easy, they are boring and not worth doing. But when they are hard, they are fun!"

Reflections on the Day

Today, students had the opportunity to continue to explore and analyze 3-D solids by their properties. If possible, continue to make the games available during choice time or indoor recess in the following weeks to allow students to continue that work. Although the games may have proved difficult for some, a conversation in the congress helped make light of just getting right answers and helped students come to appreciate the fun of challenge—one of the important CCSS Standards of Practice.

DAY NINE

CREATING A NEW BACKYARD

Materials Needed

Several sets of pattern blocks

Several sets of 3-D solids

Large chart paper or drawing paper

Writing Utensils

Paper

Today children will have the chance to use what they have learned over the last several days about two-dimensional shapes and three-dimensional solids as they design their own plans for a backyard that Baby could explore. In creating this new backyard, children will analyze and compare the properties and relationships of both two- and three-dimensional shapes, continuing to coordinate the geometries of navigation and shapes.

Day Nine Outline

Developing the Context

❖ As a whole class, create a new version of the "backyard" by tracing pattern blocks (or shape templates) and three-dimensional solids.

❖ Children work in groups to create their own "backyards" by tracing shapes.

Supporting the Investigation

❖ Note children's strategies and language as they compare and contrast two-dimensional and three-dimensional shapes.

Facilitating the Gallery Walk

❖ Conduct a brief gallery walk to allow children time to reflect and notice each other's backyards.

Developing the Context

To begin today's lesson gather the children in a circle with a large piece of paper in front of you. Tell the children that today you are going to create a new backyard for Baby to explore and brainstorm ideas together for what might be included in this new backyard (e.g. slide, sandbox, swings, playhouse, etc.). After a few minutes of brainstorming, begin placing three-dimensional solids and pattern blocks on the large blank paper and explain what each shape represents (perhaps the square pyramid is the slide and the cube is the playhouse; the sandbox could be a hexagon made out of six of the green triangles if you are using pattern blocks).

Once the shapes are placed on the paper, begin tracing the base of each three-dimensional object and have the students name the shape. For instance, the base of a cylinder is a circle, the base of a cube is a square, and the base of a rectangular prism is a rectangle. In this activity, you will introduce the names of the three-dimensional solids and encourage children to see the relationships between two-dimensional shapes and three-dimensional solids. You can encourage the children to describe the similarities and differences between these shapes and use vocabulary such as "vertices," "corners," and "sides" to describe the attributes. Once all shapes are traced, you may wish to label the places in the backyard.

Explain to children that they will work in small groups to design their own backyards. Assign groups and ensure they have all their materials available.

Supporting the Investigation

It is best for children to work in groups of three or four, no larger, as it is often difficult for young children to collaborate in larger groups. After discussing the places they want in their backyard, they can begin placing pattern blocks and three-dimensional solids on the paper. They can trace the base of each shape, color the shape, and label what that shape represents in their backyard.

You will likely see some children who struggle to trace around shapes. Their strategy may be to draw around the shape in one continuous motion, and this is difficult. Often they are using this strategy because they are still thinking of the shape topologically. You may even see them lift up the shape to finish drawing. They know the tracing needs to go around the shape, but they are not yet understanding (or making use of) the idea that the shape can be made in line segments. The development of this strategy requires children to consider edges, sides, turns, and vertices—to analyze the shape by its Euclidean properties. As you confer with these students, point out the properties using language such as edges, faces, and vertices, and suggest that making shorter lines along an edge and then turning their body when they come to vertices, before doing another edge, might help. As they shift to the use of this strategy they will become more aware of the properties of the shapes.

You may also find children you can challenge with composing and decomposing. For example you might challenge them to consider different ways to make the hexagon (six triangles, two trapezoids, etc.) or to consider if they put other shapes together to predict how many sides they will get in the new shape (three hexagons make a twelve-sided polygon—a dodecagon).

You can also support children to make use of the faces of the solids for shapes they might wish to include. For example, the cylinder base is a great template for a circle. **DO NOT JUST GIVE CHILDREN STENCILS OR ALL OF THE SHAPES THEY WANT TO TRACE.** Instead, encourage them to make use of the faces of the solids or build shapes they want from composing with others.

Facilitating the Gallery Walk

End the day with a brief Gallery Walk, where children can see the work of the other groups. Have children place their completed backyard pictures around the room. Children will have the opportunity to look around at the different backyards created and think about which shapes were used to make the footprints of the depicted objects.

Reflections on the Day

Today, children compared and contrasted two and three-dimensional shapes and used shape vocabulary. They worked on composing and decomposing shapes and continued to explore both two- and three-dimensional shapes by analyzing their properties. Tomorrow, the last day of the unit, will be spent creating a big book of adventures in the new backyards as children describe their own wild adventure stories!

DAY TEN

CREATING NEW WILD ADVENTURE STORIES

Materials Needed

Backyard Maps from Day Nine

Baby and Blankie Cut-Outs (Appendix B)

Writing utensils

Paper

Today children will tell or write their own wild adventure stories using the backyards that they created yesterday in small groups. The backyards and stories will be compiled into a class big book and children can enjoy acting out one another's stories.

Day Ten Outline

Developing the Context

❖ Tell a new Baby's Wild Adventure story with the map you made on Day Nine with the class.

❖ Ask children to work in small groups and tell and/or write their own adventure stories using their maps.

Supporting the Investigation

❖ Note children's strategies and language as they give directions and navigate the new backyard as this is a good time for assessment.

Facilitating the Math Congress

❖ Groups show their backyard maps and tell a missing Blankie story. Children can act out the stories by using the Baby and Blankie cut-outs.

❖ Make a class big book to be placed in the classroom library.

Developing the Context

Gather children together and show the backyard that was created as a whole-class in Day Nine. Using the Baby and Blankie cut-outs, work with your class to construct an adventure story. You might place Blankie on one part of the Backyard and Baby in another and have the children help you give directions so that Baby can find her Blankie and take it home. Invite a child to move the Baby cut-out as the group gives directions.

Tell children that today they will meet with their small groups and make up their own stories using their own backyard maps. Children can either write or dictate the story, which you will collect, compile, and make into a class big book.

Supporting the Investigation

Now that the unit is coming to an end, you'll want to capture the growth and development of your children—you'll want to document their mathematical journeys. Reread the Overview to the unit and examine the graphic of the landscape of learning. As you move around today and confer, think about where a child began on Day One and what you see him doing now. Have his ideas about shapes changed? Was he just doing temporal maps on Day One and now is analyzing shapes by their properties? Does he draw and give directions around shapes using line segments (forward movements) and turns? Is he able to encode the shape that is formed?

Another child may have begun on Day One making topological maps and now is able to talk about Euclidean properties like edges and faces and name and sort the 2-D shapes by their properties. She may have originally thought only the equilateral triangle was a triangle and now understands that orientation and scale don't matter: if it has 3 angles (turns) and 3 sides it is a triangle.

These are huge developmental changes and you'll want to document them. Many teachers working with the CFLM units make copies of the landscape graphic (one on each child) and highlight the landmarks on it (for example in yellow) that they have seen evidence of. In a very real sense you are documenting the journey of your young mathematicians.

Tech Tip

New Perspectives on Learning, LLC sells an assessment web-based platform that has digital versions of the landscape and the tools to attach photographs and anecdotal assessment notes. For more information go to: www.newperspectivesonlearning.com.

Facilitating the Math Congress

Instead of meeting in a whole group, you may decide to have two groups share together and take turns telling their stories. Invite groups to share their backyard maps and share their directions on finding the missing Blankie. The class can help refine any pieces of the directions that may be confusing or missing. Take photographs or scan the backyard maps and type up the children's stories to turn into a class big book. Read the class big book aloud as a final celebration of the unit and place it in the classroom library.

Reflections on the Unit

The word geometry stems from the words geo (earth) and metric (to measure). In this unit, children have had many opportunities to explore, navigate, and map the world around them. While doing so, they came to mathematize the world around them by coordinating navigation geometry with the geometry of shapes. William Smith wrote,

> The principles of Geology like those of geometry must begin at a point, through two or more of which the Geometrician draws a line and by thus proceeding from point to point, and from line to line, he constructs a map, and so proceeding from local to gen maps, and finally to a map of the world.

Initially, children were challenged to solve the "Blankie mystery," where they first explored navigation and two-dimensional shapes. Through this challenge, children drew their own representations of Baby's backyard and explored shapes as pathways that included distances and turns. Later, they were challenged to prove to the class what shapes were in Baby's Backyard. In giving directions, children had the opportunity to explore the shape of an enclosed space with properties such as distance and turns. Through games with two- and three-dimensional shapes, children sorted and identified shapes by their properties and then learned the vocabulary associated with them. Over time they came to realize that orientation, color, or scale did not define shapes; the properties did. As a culmination, children were challenged to see the relationship between two and three-dimensional shapes and designed and navigated through their own versions of Baby's backyard.

Baby's Wild Adventure

Susanna Stossel

Catherine Twomey Fosnot

Photographs by Julie A. Branby

ISBN-13: 978-1508594314
ISBN-10: 1508594317

Baby's Wild Adventure

"MamAAA! Go out!!" Baby banged on the door. She had been waiting all morning to go outside to play. She was getting very impatient and now the phone was ringing.

"Just a minute!" called Momma. "Where did I put that phone... Oh, Hi Ellen. How are you?"

Baby hated the phone. Baby banged on the door again, then crawled to find her Blankie.

"Thwap, thwap!" What was that noise? Baby crawled over to investigate. It was a shape on the back door in the kitchen, and it was moving!

Just then Tiger, their cat, came through the shape. "Thwap, thwap."

"That moves?" wondered Baby. She crawled over and touched the shape. "That OPENS?" marveled Baby as she pushed on the shape.

"OUTSIDE!" said Baby as she stuck her head through the door. She dragged Blankie with her and crawled outside.

This was amazing! Baby LOVED outside. There was so much to see and hear and smell. Baby crawled straight along a path of very tall flowers.

Flitting in and out of the flowers was a beautiful butterfly.

Baby wanted to pat the butterfly. She dropped Blankie to reach up as tall as she could, standing for a very quick, very wobbly moment. "BaFly!"

The butterfly started to fly away. Baby crawled some more, straight along the edge of the meadow with the flowers. The butterfly turned a corner to visit a sunflower. Baby crawled around the corner as well. The butterfly kept flying in and out of the yellow flowers, then disappeared. Baby went straight for a bit more and turned another corner and found the butterfly again. She just wanted to pat those beautiful colors but the butterfly flew on. Was it gone? Baby went straight some more and then turned another corner and found it again.

"BaFly!" she called to the butterfly and crawled straight after it. The butterfly disappeared again, this time around some blue flowers. "BaFly?" Baby turned another corner and saw the butterfly again. She crawled after it but the butterfly flew up and Baby couldn't see it anymore because of the sun. Baby was sad to see the butterfly go.

But, wait a minute! Here was Blankie! How could that be? She had gone on 4 straight paths and turned 4 corners! How could she be back near Blankie?

Baby grabbed Blankie and kept crawling. Then Baby saw something interesting! Another Blankie? No, it was a yellow toad in a field of vegetables!

Baby wanted to catch the toad even more than the butterfly. She crawled over to the field. She reached out both hands to catch the toad and dropped Blankie again!

Hop! Toad hopped out of sight behind the zucchini.

Baby crawled straight down the long vegetable path after Toad and went around the same corner as Toad. And there was Toad! But Toad made three big hops. Baby tried to catch up. She wished that she could make big jumps like Toad, but she didn't know how, so she crawled and crawled down another straight path, along the field of vegetables.

What a big farm it was! Soon she was almost to Toad. She reached out. Hop! Toad turned a second corner and disappeared again! Finally Baby reached the corner and peeked around. There was Toad! But just when Baby crawled around and got close enough to touch Toad, hop! Hop! Hop! Hop! All the way to the end of the tomatoes and peppers!

Baby crawled quietly, straight some more, on and on, getting closer and closer. Baby was almost to Toad! She reached out and touched the tip of Toad. HOP! Toad jumped straight up in the air and then bounced around a third corner. So Baby turned around the corner. Toad made 4 big jumps again and started nibbling. What was Toad nibbling on? Was that Blankie?

Baby crawled as fast as she could. "No, no, NO!" Baby yelled to Toad and chased Toad away from Blankie. She picked up Blankie and hugged it. It wasn't lost after all, not even after 3 straight paths and 3 corners! Baby crawled to a safer spot. Whew!

But now Baby was feeling hot. What was that in the distance? It looked like a big, big lake. Maybe that would cool her off. She would go for a swim.

Baby was not allowed to swim without Momma, but maybe she could just splash a little bit. She crawled over to the water. It looked so refreshing and inviting! She crawled right to the edge of the water, put Blankie down beside her, and patted the water with both hands. Splash, splash. Oh, that was fun! Splash, splash! Baby loved this lake.

Baby splashed some water on a rock. What? That rock has a head? And feet? Yikes! It's moving! It's a turtle! Baby splashed Turtle again. But Turtle didn't like the splashing and started crawling away, along the shore.

Baby liked following Turtle. The lake had no corners! It was much easier than following Butterfly and Toad! Baby stopped every few minutes to splash a little bit but was still able to catch up to Turtle. Baby chased Turtle all the way around the lake! Oops! Turtle got tired of being chased around the lake and went right in for a swim. Oh, Baby was sad to see Turtle go.

But look! Is that another turtle? No, it is Blankie! But where did Blankie come from? How could it be here? Baby had put it down when she first saw Turtle! No corners even! She had just gone around the lake.

With all of this water around, Baby was starting to feel thirsty. Where could she find something to drink? She began to wish she had waited for Momma. How would she ever find her way home? Then, in the distance, behind the meadow with the flowers and just in front of the woods, Baby thought she saw a cabin. Was this her house? Would Momma be there waiting for her?

She dropped Blankie in excitement, and pulled herself up to standing. Should she go to the woods alone? She was afraid, but she had to see if it was her house. She had to find Momma. So Baby went to the cabin near the woods.

Bang, bang! Baby tried knocking, but no one answered. Using the walls for support Baby toddled along one wall of the cabin.

She came to the end. Should she go around the corner? Yes! She did it! Baby tried banging again. Still no answer! Baby edged along this second wall to another corner! Baby wobbled but didn't fall. She was getting faster on her feet. This time she banged along the whole wall AND the next corner. Baby was getting tired. She slowed down as she padded along the wall. Another corner? Baby stepped around it then...BOOM!

Baby fell down but it didn't hurt, because somehow, she fell on Blankie! She had gone along 4 sides of the cabin and turned 4 corners! How did Blankie get here?

She couldn't find her house or Momma, but at least she had Blankie. Baby sat down in the shade under a kumquat tree. She was hot and tired and she didn't know which way to go. The tree was on the edge of a jungle and Baby thought she better not go any further until she rested and thought about what to do. She picked some of the orange fruit. They tasted a little bit like oranges. Baby liked them and soon she felt better.

Just then Baby heard a loud, scary sound, "CROAK."

What was that? Baby didn't want to find out. She
dropped Blankie and started crawling as fast as she could
straight along the edge of the jungle in the shade. Then Baby
saw Tiger run by and disappear. Maybe Tiger could show
Baby the way home?

Baby decided to follow him. She looked around the corner and saw Tiger's tail. She chased after it but it disappeared again. At the end of the path Baby saw a second corner and looked around it just in time to see Tiger disappear into the deep dark jungle.

Baby followed around the corner, and to the spot where Tiger had gone, but she did not want to go into the jungle. She just wanted to go home. Along the edge of the path,

Baby saw another corner – maybe Tiger would be around that turn? Baby went around that corner. No Tiger. Baby kept going but she wanted Momma!

"Momma?" Baby called, "Momma!?"

"Baby! I'm right here!" Baby crawled along the edge of the jungle and peeked her head around the 4th corner. There was Momma holding Blankie. She crawled into her arms. How did Momma get Blankie?

"How is my little adventurer?" Momma kissed Baby's head and picked her up. "Do you want some juice?" Baby clutched Blankie and nodded yes, but by the time Momma carried her into the house, she was already fast asleep.

A Map of Baby's Backyard

Appendix B

(Cut around each shape and glue to oaktag. To make Baby stand, you can hold her up in a wooden clip clothespin.)

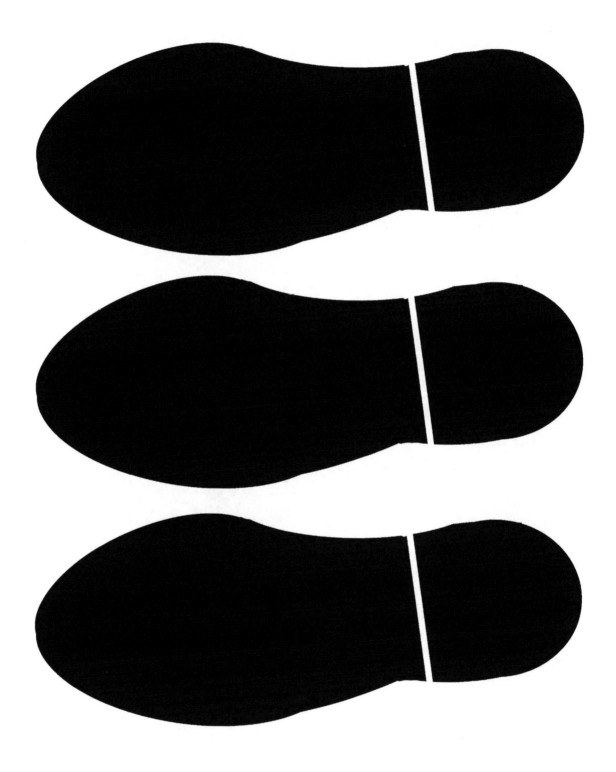

Vegetable Garden

3 _____

3 Turns

What shape is it?

The Lake

0 _____

Baby just went around it.

What shape is it?

The Cabin

4 _____

4 Turns

What shape is it?

The Jungle

4 _____

4 Turns

What shape is it?

On the side of

In front of

Behind

By the corner of

Next to

Under

These shapes can be enlarged so that there is one per piece of paper.

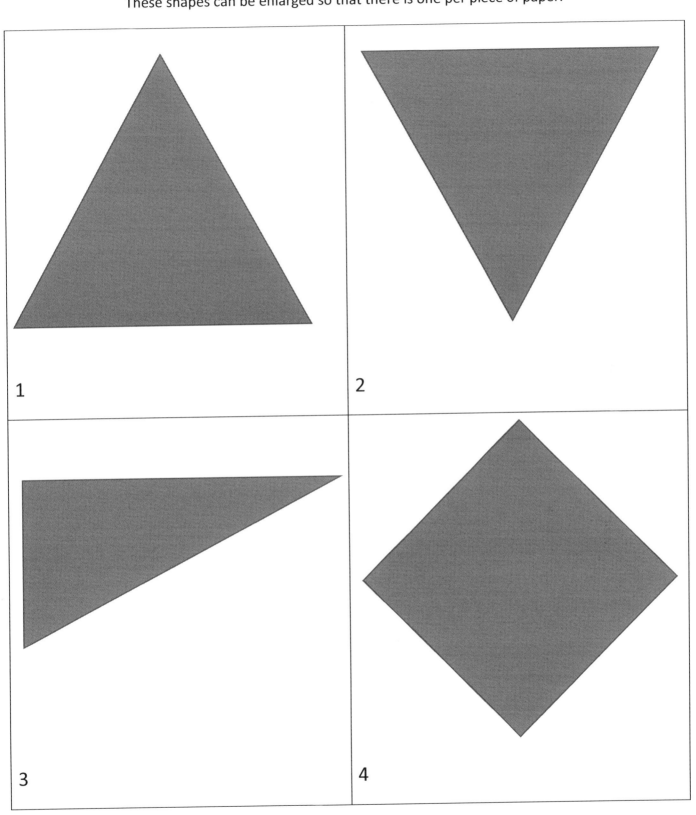

1

2

3

4

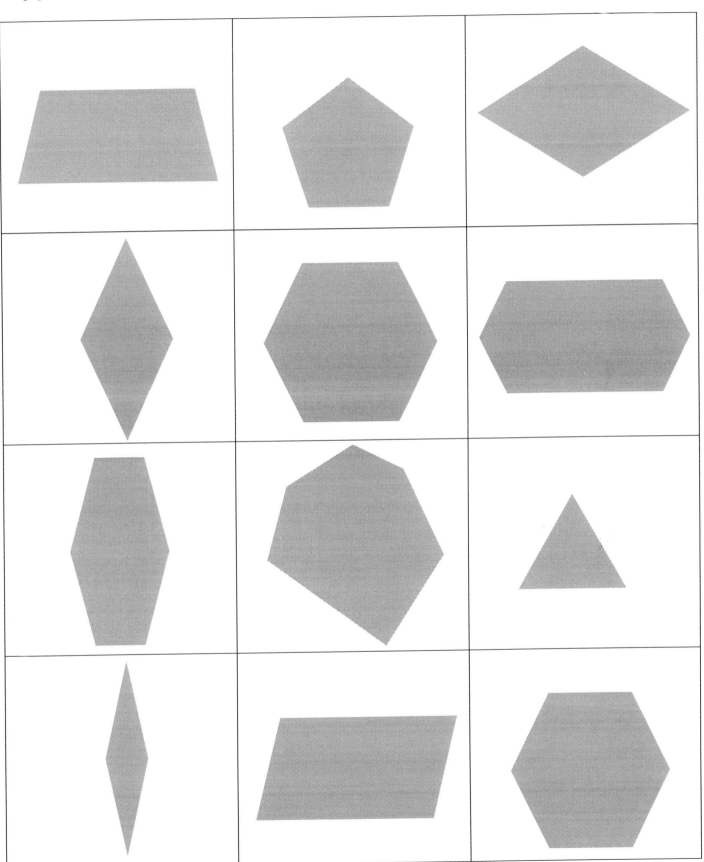

3 STRAIGHTS 3 TURNS	3 STRAIGHTS 3 TURNS	3 STRAIGHTS 3 TURNS
3 STRAIGHTS 3 TURNS	4 STRAIGHTS 4 TURNS	4 STRAIGHTS 4 TURNS
4 STRAIGHTS 4 TURNS	4 STRAIGHTS 4 TURNS	5 STRAIGHTS 5 TURNS
5 STRAIGHTS 5 TURNS	6 STRAIGHTS 6 TURNS	6 STRAIGHTS 6 TURNS

Direction card:

Drawing of the shape we made with footprints:

Made in the USA
Middletown, DE
11 October 2016